TRAVELING

TRAVELING

Getting Around on a
Very Small Planet

A word to Parents:

All of the activities in this book have been successfully performed by children. The ease with which these have been accomplished has varied with the age and skill development of each individual child. A project which is both safe and easy for a twelve-year-old, may require adult supervision for a child of eight. Basic rules of safety apply to all children and should be scrupulously followed in whatever they do. Only you, the parents, can determine the ease with which your children can successfully and safely perform any activity. Only you can determine the degree of guidance your children will require.

This is not a book to *read*—it is a book to *do*.

We have designed this book to be enjoyed by all ages. We hope that it will provide many hours of pleasure for you and your children.

The Editors

Contents

HERE TO THERE 99

COMIN' HOME 117

by yourself

Ready...

ANSWER an invitation to visit a friend or a cousin. Find out the days you will visit and some things you will do. Tell your friend exactly how you will arrive. Give the name of the station or airport, the date, and the time. Give the flight number if you are traveling by airplane. You may have to write two or three letters. Make sure everyone understands the details.

ARRANGE a family meeting to work out the cost of your trip. Call a travel agency, train station, or airport. Find out the cost of transportation. Figure out what meals you will eat along the way. Decide how much to spend for each meal. Talk about the things you will do when you visit. Your friends or relatives will pay for your meals. You may pay for extras such as movies and swimming. Total all these expenses. Add a little more for emergencies.

EARN part of the money yourself. Find ways to earn money.

DECIDE what clothes to take along. Wear nice clothes for traveling. Good pants, shirt, or blouse and sweater are appropriate for both girls and boys. Try to take along clothes that don't need ironing. Or learn to iron your own clothes. Remember, you will have to carry your own suitcase. Limit yourself to one suitcase that you can carry.

THINK about the length of your visit. Take clothes for every day of a short visit. For a long visit, take enough to last a week. Be prepared to do your own laundry.

THINK about the weather and what you will do. Take a raincoat and swim suit for a summer trip. Take a parka and boots for a winter ski trip.

REMEMBER to pack a toothbrush, underwear, and the other things you normally use. Make a list of all these things.

SAFARI PACKING LIST
2 Pair jeans ✓
2 Pair shorts ✓
3 Pair shoes
1 Bathing suit
7 Pair underwear
Pair Socks
1 Dress
1 Safari
5 Shirts
4 P

9

Go!!!

FIND your way around a station, depot, or airport. Look for signs with arrows. They point the way to the rest room, train track, or airline gate. Search for the Travelers' Aid Society. They can answer any question and handle any emergency. Find the information booth. They can answer questions. Don't worry when you're really lost. Find a policeman or someone who works in the station. They will be happy to answer your questions.

AVOID talking to strangers. Stay in the main areas of the station. Never tell a stranger your name or address. If necessary, make up a name and address. Talk about general topics such as the weather or sports. Never accept a gift or let a stranger pay for meals. Tell a stranger you need to check on your train or plane. Then move away.

USE your common sense. Most people are very nice. Kids your own age are fine. Let a little old lady tell you about her grandchildren.

Artful Arrivals

FIND OUT what time you will arrive. Check your schedule, or wait for the stewardess or conductor to tell you. Use the rest room several minutes before your arrival. It may take a long time to get in the station and collect your luggage.

CHECK for all your belongings. Make sure you take everything with you. Take your ticket and baggage claim too. Ask another passenger to help take things off the rack.

LOOK for your friends or relatives at the gate. Wait a few minutes if you don't see them. It's easy to be delayed by traffic.

GO to the information desk if no one meets you. Tell them the name of your friends or relatives. The people at the desk will call for them over the loudspeaker. Wait a long time for them to find the information desk.

INFORMATION DESK

WHeeLs

CALL the bus depot several days before your trip. Sometimes you need to reserve a ticket. Arrive at the depot half an hour before the departure time. Buy your ticket at the ticket window. Find out the gate number for your bus.

GO to the correct gate. Give a large suitcase to the driver. He will put a number on it and give you a claim check. He will put your suitcase in the luggage section under the bus. At the end of the trip, give the driver your claim check. He will give you the suitcase.

CHOOSE a good seat on the bus. The middle seats are the most comfortable. Take a front seat if you get motion sickness. Look out the front window.

KEEP things you will use on the seat. A book and snacks are fine. Place other things on the rack over your seat. Ask another passenger to help you reach the rack.

ADJUST your seat so that it is comfortable. Push the button on the arm of the seat. Push the seat back, or let it come forward. Release the button when the seat is in position. Adjust the foot rest. Lift it to a higher position. Push the lever to make it go down.

FIND the rest room in the back of the bus. Look at the label above the handle. A red label says "occupied" when someone is inside. A blue label says "vacant" when no one is inside. Wait for your turn. When you are inside, adjust the label to "occupied."

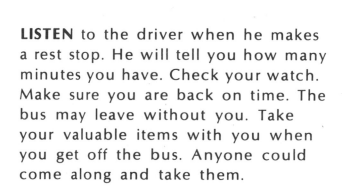

LISTEN to the driver when he makes a rest stop. He will tell you how many minutes you have. Check your watch. Make sure you are back on time. The bus may leave without you. Take your valuable items with you when you get off the bus. Anyone could come along and take them.

TELL the driver if you feel sick. He knows just what to do.

Rails

CALL the train station when you plan your trip. Find out if you need a reservation. Ask what time the train leaves.

ARRIVE at the station twenty or thirty minutes early. Look for the ticket window and buy your ticket. Find out the track number for your train. Ask the ticket seller, look at the bulletin board, or listen to the loudspeaker.

FIND your way to the right track, and take a seat on the train. Decide where to put your luggage. Put it on the rack over your seat. Ask someone to help you reach the rack. Or find the luggage section at the end of the car. It is a metal bin. Set your suitcase inside. Some trains have a baggage car. Find the baggage check place inside the station. Give the person your suitcase. He will put a tag on it and give you a baggage check. Keep it with your ticket.

EXPLORE for buttons and levers on your seat. It will adjust like a bus seat. Some trains have reading lamps. Locate the button next to the lamp. Turn it on or off. Lower the curtain when you want a nap. Find the lever at one end of the curtain. Press the two sections together. Do the same thing at the other end of the curtain. Then raise or lower it. You may share a window with someone. Ask permission before you adjust the curtain.

WATCH for the conductor to come through the train. Give him your ticket. He will give it back to you or clip it to the seat in front of you. Take the ticket if you leave your seat. It is proof that you bought a ticket.

FIND the rest rooms. The men's room is at one end of the car. The women's room is at the other end. Many trains have a drinking fountain. Use the small paper cup. Fill it only part way so you won't spill.

15

ENJOY a lunch on the train. It's fun to take a sack lunch with you. Some trains have food vendors. They walk down the aisle to sell snacks. Other trains have a snack bar. Ask the conductor where it is. Walk carefully between train cars. The doors are quite heavy. Find a handle, and hold on. Buy soft drinks, sandwiches, and other snacks. You will get them in a small box. Carry it back to your seat.

FIND OUT if your train has a diner. The food is more expensive, but it's fun. When the food is ready, a porter will come to your car. He will ring a bell to announce that dinner is ready. Walk carefully to the diner. Wait inside the door. Someone will take you to a table. Write your order on the check. Try not to spill food. Put a spoon in a cup or bowl. Fill your glass only part way. Pay for your meal when you are finished.

LOOK for an observation car at the end of your train. It has huge windows to let you enjoy the view. You may like to stand up and move around for a change. Some trains have a club car. It is a place for people to smoke, play cards, and have a drink. It is best to leave that car for adults.

TAKE your valuable things with you whenever you leave your seat. Make sure you have your ticket, baggage check, and money.

PREPARE yourself to get off at your stop. The conductor will tell you when you have a few more minutes. Collect everything around your seat. Remember the baggage claim. Take the suitcase off the rack after the train is at a complete stop.

LOOK for your friends and relatives. They will wait on the platform of a small station. At a large station, follow the other passengers who get off. Meet your friends at the entrance to the main building.

Wings

CALL the airport several days before your flight. Make a reservation.

PACK your clothes carefully. The airline will let you take three suitcases. The two big ones will go in the baggage section. You must carry the small one on the plane. Measure the length, width, and depth of your suitcase. Add the numbers. The suitcases must be no bigger than 62, 55, and 45 inches.

ALLOW plenty of time for your family to take you to the airport. Be inside the airport half an hour before your departure time. Go to the section that has the name of your airline. Get in line at the ticket counter. Pay for your ticket and turn over your suitcases. You will receive a ticket and a claim check for each suitcase. Ask for the flight number of your plane.

FLIGHT NUMBER	GATE NUMBER	TIME OF DEPARTURE
RRA 210	D6	11:00 AM
RRA 111	D8	2:00 PM
RRA 302	D10	9:00 PM

CHECK your flight number on the bulletin board. It will tell you the gate number and departure time. Listen for the same information off the loudspeaker. In bad weather the plane may leave late.

FOLLOW the signs to your gate. Stop at the safety check. Give everything you are carrying to the person at the counter. Walk through the arch. Pick up your things on the other side.

WAIT at the gate for your plane. Someone will check your ticket. When the gate opens, walk on the ramp to the plane. Your family will wave from the gate.

CHOOSE a comfortable seat. The front section is first class and more expensive. Walk through the curtain to the back section. The seats in the middle of the plane give the smoothest ride. The back gets rather bouncy. Find the best view just in front of or behind the wing.

PUT your suitcase under your seat. Only soft things, like a coat, can go up on the rack. On a rough ride, a falling suitcase is unpleasant. Adjust your seat as you did on the bus or train. Find the air vent above your head. Turn the center section around to turn it on or off. Find the button to call the stewardess. When you turn it on she will see a light. Look for a sign at the front of the plane. When the light goes on, buckle your seat belt. Look in the pocket in front of your seat. Find directions for all the buttons and levers.

RELAX when the plane begins to move. The vibrations and noises are normal. The plane will rock back and forth when the engines start.

TAKE some gum or candy when the stewardess comes by. Your ears can plug up when the plane takes off. Yawning, swallowing, and chewing gum will help.

WATCH the sign at the front of the plane. When the light goes off, unbuckle your seat belt. Get up and walk around the plane. A drinking fountain and magazine rack will be at one end. The rest rooms are at the back. They have an "occupied" and a "vacant" sign similar to the bus. Listen for the loudspeaker. When the ride gets rough, the stewardess will tell you to go back and fasten your seat belt.

WAIT for the stewardess to bring your meal. She is very busy and will give you only one chance to take a tray.

RELAX if you begin to feel sick. You are probably just nervous. Adjust the air vent. A little cool air helps. Call the stewardess to help you. If you are going to be sick, use the bag in the seat flap.

TAKE all your belongings when the plane lands. Your friends will meet you at the gate. Walk with them to the baggage claim.

Cool Company

CALL your friend's parents by Mr. and Mrs. Use their first names only when they suggest it. Try to get along with little children. When they bother you, get them interested in something else. Be friends with the family dog too.

FIND OUT about your sleeping arrangements. Your friend will show you to the bedroom. Find the closet for your clothes and your towels in the bathroom. Don't expect too much of a summer cabin. Your bed may be a cot in the corner.

FIT into the family eating schedule. Ask what you may take for snacks. Get dressed for the first breakfast. If the others are in bathrobes, you may wear yours too. Wait to be seated at the table. Most people have a regular seat. Take one bite of every food on the table. Some new foods will be very good. But don't make yourself sick eating too much. Ask permission before taking a second helping.

TRY not to get up very early. The noise will bother other people. Keep a book by the bed. Read until the others are up and around. Remember to make your bed.

SHARE the bathroom with the family. It is polite to let the family have it first in the morning. Keep your toothbrush and shampoo out of the way. Always knock on a closed door before you enter.

HELP with the household chores. Ask for things that you can do. Take care of your own laundry. Someone will show you how to use the machine.

TAKE good care of sports equipment. Keep it clean and put away. Ask permission before using complicated equipment.

ASK for permission before changing TV stations and before making long distance phone calls.

TAKE all of your belongings with you when you go home. Thank the family for a good time.

23

Traveler's Treasure

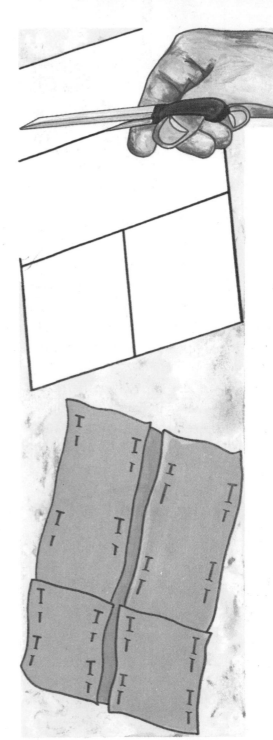

KEEP important traveling papers together. Make a folder for your emergency phone numbers, tickets, and baggage claims. Carry the folder in your pocket or purse.

FIND some large pieces of felt and some smaller scraps. Get strong thread, needle, scissors, paper, pencil, glue, yarn, ruler, and pins.

DRAW three rectangles on the paper. Use the ruler to keep the lines straight. Make one 9 by 7-1/2 inches, another 9 by 3-1/2 inches and another 3-1/2 by 3-1/2 inches.

PIN a rectangle on a piece of felt. Cut around the edge of the paper. Cut one large rectangle and two of each small rectangle. You will have five rectangles.

PLACE the 9 by 3-1/2 inch rectangles on top of the large one. Put the small rectangles in the corners.

MAKE SURE the pieces are straight. Pin them together.

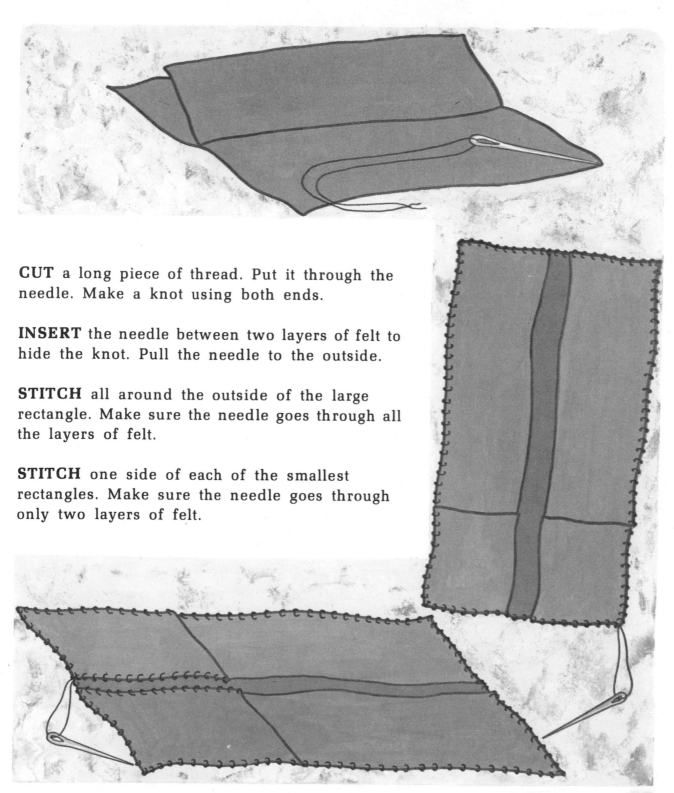

CUT a long piece of thread. Put it through the needle. Make a knot using both ends.

INSERT the needle between two layers of felt to hide the knot. Pull the needle to the outside.

STITCH all around the outside of the large rectangle. Make sure the needle goes through all the layers of felt.

STITCH one side of each of the smallest rectangles. Make sure the needle goes through only two layers of felt.

DRAW a clown's head, eyes, nose, and mouth on a piece of paper. Make sure the eyes are a little bigger than a dime. Cut out each piece.

PIN the eyes to the head. Carefully stitch around them. Cut a line through each eye.

SPREAD glue on the back of the nose and mouth. Glue them to the head.

CUT about six pieces of yarn. Put them together. Take another piece of yarn and tie it around the middle. Spread some glue on the yarn. Glue it to the head.

SPREAD glue on the back of the head. Attach it to the outside of the traveler's treasure.

COLLECT your money, emergency phone numbers, tickets, and baggage claims. Put them in the pockets. Get two dimes for phone calls. Put them in the clown's eyes.

Roughing It

Camper's Choice

CHOOSE a good camp for you. Church camps and scout camps are good. Find a camp for your special interests. Do you prefer music or horses? Talk to friends who went to camp last summer. They will help you find a good camp.

COLLECT information from the camp. One form shows the dates of the camp sessions. Choose the time you want to go to camp and return the form. Another paper is a doctor's certificate. Take it to your family doctor. He will fill it out and give it back to you. Remember to take it to camp. Another paper is a list of clothing. Check it carefully. Make sure you have everything on the list. Old clothes are great for roughing it.

FIND a pen with indelible ink. Write your name on all your clothes for camp. The ink won't wash off in the laundry.

DECIDE what else to take to camp. You may want a camera or stationery. Take paperback books and not library books. Rain is a wrinkler.

Roomy Roll

FIND a waterproof canvas or piece of plastic, two blankets, a sheet, and a strong rope.

LAY the plastic on the ground.

PLACE a blanket half on the plastic.

PUT a second blanket in the middle of the plastic.

FOLD a sheet in half. Put it in the middle.

START with the sheet. Fold each blanket over in the middle. Fold over the plastic.

ROLL UP the blankets. Tie a rope around them.

Settle In

LOOK for the counselors at the camp entrance. Tell them your name. One of them will take you to your tent or cabin.

HAUL your things into the cabin. Choose an empty bed, and fix up your bedroll. Find a good place to keep your suitcase and hooks for hanging things. Check the nearby buildings. Find out where you will wash up.

TAKE a tour of the camp. Ask a new cabinmate to come along. Find the location for your camp activities. Is there a lake or pool? Where will you eat? Find the nurse's station and the camp store.

LEARN the camp schedule. A camp counselor will explain it to you. Bells or other signals will tell you the time.

JOIN the counselor for the first meal. Each camp has its own style. Sit at your own table. Learn the table manners. Take your turn doing each job. The first night you may serve food.

ENJOY the first campfire. Sing along with the camp songs, and try the games. The counselors will provide good entertainment.

EXPECT only a little sleep the first night. Everyone will be very excited and will want to talk. The woods will be filled with strange sounds. An owl will hoot, or a mouse will scurry under the tent. With luck, you'll have a thunder storm. The good sleeping begins the second night.

Getting Along

MAKE new friends at camp. Start with the people in your tent or cabin. Think of a good question to start a conversation. Be friendly and cheerful. Make friends with a shy person. Respect your tentmates. Do your best to be neat and to get along.

TRY all the camp activities. You'll like some new things. Your friends like a good sport. Camp is for having a good time. Relax and enjoy yourself.

LEARN to handle homesickness. It happens to many people, so don't be ashamed. It's hard to be in a completely new place. Make a calendar on a piece of notepaper. Cross off each day when you go to bed. Your stay at camp is really very short. Try to keep busy. Think of one fantastic thing that has happened each day.

VISIT the nurse if you have an accident or feel sick. She will fix you up in no time.

Fond Farewells

MAKE your last day special. Have a fantastic last swim. Remember all your best times.

GET OUT your notebook and pencil. Collect autographs from the counselors and your friends. Remember to get the addresses of your best friends. Write letters until next summer.

INCLUDE other things in your notebook. Write down the words to the camp songs. Include directions for your favorite camp crafts. Leave room to put in photographs.

COLLECT all your belongings. Roll up the bedroll. Make sure you remember everything.

Camper's Case

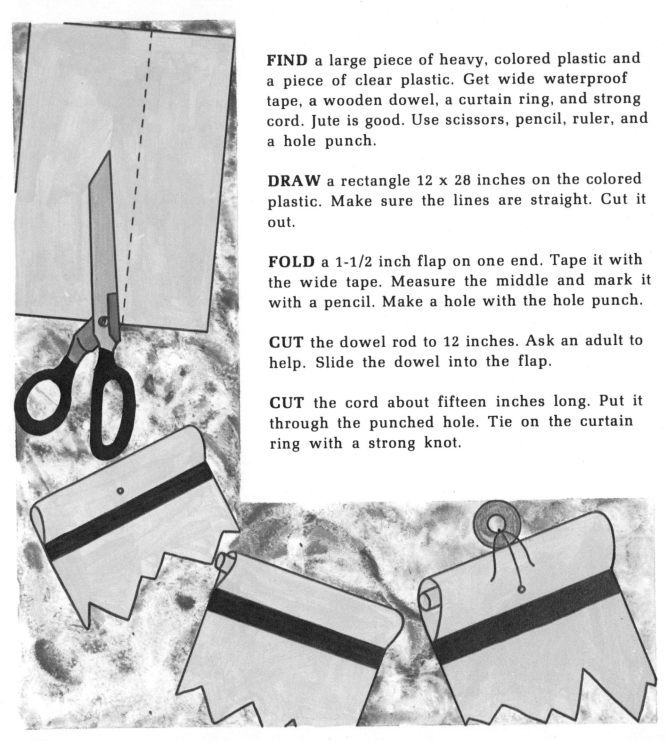

FIND a large piece of heavy, colored plastic and a piece of clear plastic. Get wide waterproof tape, a wooden dowel, a curtain ring, and strong cord. Jute is good. Use scissors, pencil, ruler, and a hole punch.

DRAW a rectangle 12 x 28 inches on the colored plastic. Make sure the lines are straight. Cut it out.

FOLD a 1-1/2 inch flap on one end. Tape it with the wide tape. Measure the middle and mark it with a pencil. Make a hole with the hole punch.

CUT the dowel rod to 12 inches. Ask an adult to help. Slide the dowel into the flap.

CUT the cord about fifteen inches long. Put it through the punched hole. Tie on the curtain ring with a strong knot.

DRAW a rectangle 5 x 11 inches on the clear plastic. Cut it out. Make three more rectangles the same size.

PLACE the first rectangle at the top of the colored plastic. Cut a piece of tape 12 inches long. Try not to let it twist. Tape down the bottom side of the rectangle.

PUT another rectangle under the first one. Tape the bottom edge. Do the same thing with the other rectangles.

START at the top of the plastic. Carefully roll the tape down the rectangles. One piece will hold all four edges.

PUT another long piece of tape down the other side.

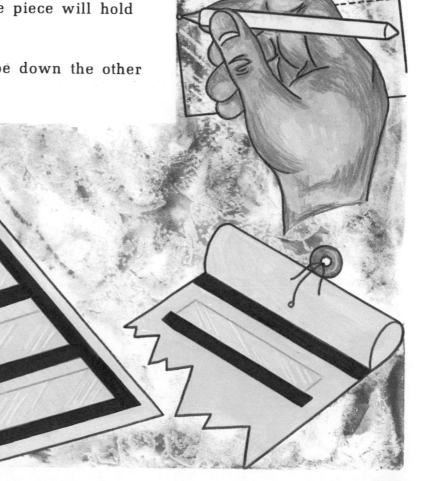

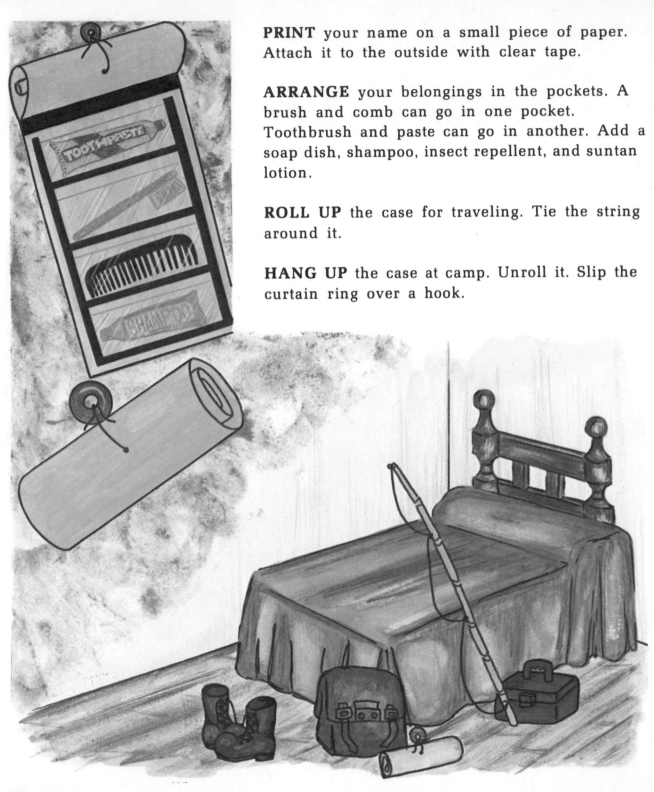

PRINT your name on a small piece of paper. Attach it to the outside with clear tape.

ARRANGE your belongings in the pockets. A brush and comb can go in one pocket. Toothbrush and paste can go in another. Add a soap dish, shampoo, insect repellent, and suntan lotion.

ROLL UP the case for traveling. Tie the string around it.

HANG UP the case at camp. Unroll it. Slip the curtain ring over a hook.

minitrips

Uptown, Downtown

STAY in the city for one-day vacations.

USE buses, subways, bikes, and feet to get to your destination.

PACK a brown bag lunch for these short trips.

VISIT the library first. Get a list of museums, art galleries, and other special places in your city. Write down the hours they are open. Find out if there are admission fees.

DECIDE which places to visit. You might be able to take a one-day trip each week.

TRIP to the zoo! That's for you!

VISIT the farmers' market. Is there a fish market in your city? It will be a fun and fragrant trip. Whew.

TAKE a trip to the police and fire departments. Ask for a tour of each.

PLAN a visit to a large newspaper office. Ask to see the various departments. Safety rules might keep you out of some of them.

GO to a baseball game. Make it a double-header.

KEEP a list of all the one-day trips you make. Keep another list of the places you want to go.

Who needs a six-month world cruise?

A Day Away

GET a map of your state. Find your town. Check the legend to find out how many miles equal an inch of map space.

USE your town as a circle's center. Draw a circle around your town. The circle should be three inches across.

MAKE a list of all the towns, parks, or special places that are in the circle.

TALK with the rest of the family. Agree on some places to visit that are on the list. These can be one-day trips.

READ your newspaper. Look for events that will be held within the circled area.

CALL the local historical society. Ask them for a list of interesting places near your town.

WRITE to Chambers of Commerce in nearby towns. Ask if there will be fairs, horse shows, or circuses going on.

TELEPHONE the nearest Farm Bureau office. Find out if there are any large dairy or cattle farms within your circle. You might want to visit one.

TRY tours of manufacturing plants. Auto factories, glass makers, and cereal factories are some to explore. Call or write each plant for tour information.

THINK about other one-day jaunts. Visit a major airport. You might get to tour a jumbo jet.

TAKE a walking tour of a university. Most of them have museums. Some have planetariums or observatories.

TRY a family canoe trip.

GO fishing.

Or?

CITY MUSEUM

Weekends Off

PLAN a two or three-day vacation.

WRITE to your state travel bureau. Ask for a list of farms or ranches who accept guests. A weekend in the country is very nice. You might get to help gather eggs.

WATCH the newspapers for berry or fruit festivals. These give you a chance to camp for a couple of days. Bringing home blueberries or cherries is the best part.

LEARN about neighboring states.

ASK an auto club to give you information about the state next door. Figure out how far you could travel into that state. What things do you want to see and do?

TRY a weekend in a motel with indoor pool. You can spend time splashing and diving. There might be shuffleboard courts inside. Make friends with other kids staying there. You might get a new pen pal or three.

SPEND a couple of days at a state fair.

FIND OUT if colleges near you offer weekend workshops. Your whole family might like to join an art, pottery, or photography workshop.

TAKE a photo journey in autumn. Drive through areas with the best fall colors. Take lots of pictures. Enter your best one in an amateur contest.

HAVE a cozy weekend. Spend it with grandparents. Go for walks. Help bake bread. Do some odd jobs.

Share yourself.

Minimoney

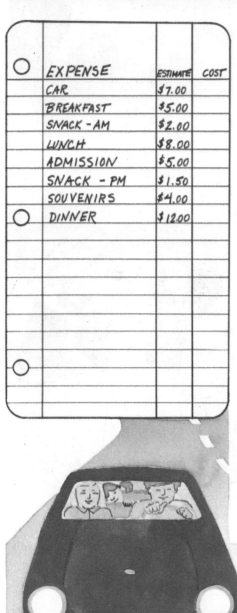

EXPENSE	ESTIMATE	COST
CAR	$7.00	
BREAKFAST	$5.00	
SNACK - AM	$2.00	
LUNCH	$8.00	
ADMISSION	$5.00	
SNACK - PM	$1.50	
SOUVENIRS	$4.00	
DINNER	$12.00	

FIGURE OUT a budget for each minitrip you make.

MAKE a chart showing what you think the trip will cost.

WRITE DOWN the cost of gasoline. Ask dad how many miles per gallon of gas your car will go. Divide those miles into the total miles you are going to travel. Multiply the answer by the cost of one gallon of gas. This will give you an estimate of gasoline costs.

FIGURE OUT how many meals your family will eat on the outing. Write down what you think the meals will cost.

GUESS how much will be spent for admission tickets. Also note how much you think will be spent on souvenirs.

LIST how much might be spent for parking fees or emergencies.

TAKE a pencil and paper on the trip.

JOT DOWN every amount of money spent and what it was for. Be sure to record everything.

COMPARE what was spent with what you thought would be. Did you go over or under?

LOOK at the biggest amount spent. What was it for? Perhaps most of the money went for snacks or meals.

PRINT the actual cost of each thing next to the estimated cost on your chart.

SHOW your parents your chart. Tell them how you made it.

OFFER ways to save money on the next minitrip your family takes.

SUGGEST that the family eat breakfast before leaving home the next time.

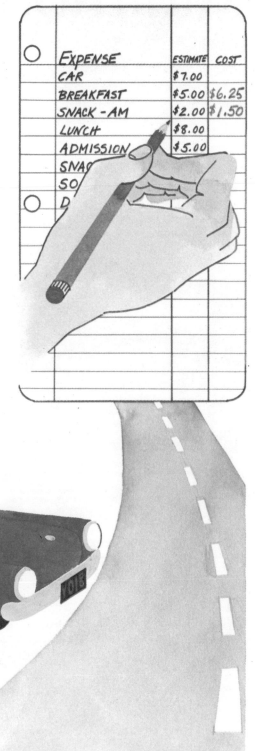

EXPENSE	ESTIMATE	COST
CAR	$7.00	
BREAKFAST	$5.00	$6.25
SNACK - AM	$2.00	$1.50
LUNCH	$8.00	
ADMISSION	$5.00	
SNA		
SO		
D		

PICNIC instead of eating in restaurants.

ALLOW a set amount of spending money for each kid. Everyone understands that he can spend only that amount. No more.

TAKE fruit drink in an insulated jug. The cost of soft drinks can be saved.

You might be able to save enough to have an extra minitrip next year.

Planning Session

SET UP a meeting for the family to plan the vacation.

TALK about the dates of the trip. Decide whether there will be time for sightseeing along the way. Or will you have to hurry to get to one place?

MAKE a list of the states you will go through.

FIGURE OUT how much money the vacation will cost.

WRITE DOWN how many nights the family will spend in motels or hotels. How many nights will you stay with friends or relatives?

TRY to add up the number of meals the family will eat in restaurants.

CALL several motels in your town. Ask each one how much a one-night stay costs for a family your size. This will give you an idea of what it will cost for lodging on your trip.

VISIT some restaurants in your town. Order at least a soft drink. Read the menu carefully. Write down the most expensive and cheapest breakfasts and prices. Do the same for lunches and dinners.

PUT your motel and meal price notes in an envelope.

Finding Out

GET some stationery and stamps. Use your best handwriting.

WRITE to places where you will be traveling. Find out if there will be special events while you are there. You should get free information.

SEND letters to state travel bureaus at each state's capital. You can get correct addresses at the library.

WRITE to the Chamber of Commerce in each city you plan to visit. Ask for city maps and tourist information.

LEARN more about state parks. Ask for information about them from the state park commissions in each state.

ASK your librarian for the address to write for information on national parks and federal recreation areas.

VISIT service stations in your town. Ask for addresses of their oil companies' tourist information offices. Write to them.

COPY the following letter to ask for information. Be sure to use the right address. Don't forget to put in your name and address.

Date

Name
Street or P.O. Box
City, State, Zip Code

Gentlemen:

My family and I will be in _____ during the month of _____. Please send me maps and information about things we can see and do there.

Thank you very much.

Sincerely yours,
Mary Ellen Gardner
820 Oxford Road
Ann Arbor, Mich.
48104

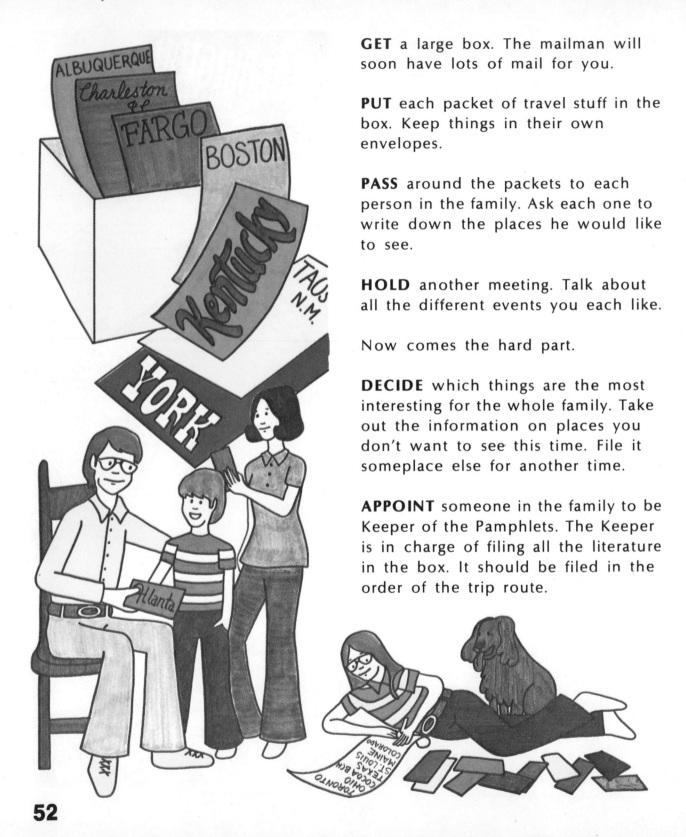

GET a large box. The mailman will soon have lots of mail for you.

PUT each packet of travel stuff in the box. Keep things in their own envelopes.

PASS around the packets to each person in the family. Ask each one to write down the places he would like to see.

HOLD another meeting. Talk about all the different events you each like.

Now comes the hard part.

DECIDE which things are the most interesting for the whole family. Take out the information on places you don't want to see this time. File it someplace else for another time.

APPOINT someone in the family to be Keeper of the Pamphlets. The Keeper is in charge of filing all the literature in the box. It should be filed in the order of the trip route.

DON'T FORGET to take the box.

ELECT a Trip Treasurer at the meeting. His job is to know how much each event will cost. He asks the Keeper. The Trip Treasurer can hold the money needed each day to get into museums or parks. The Treasurer might be in charge of snack or souvenir funds each day.

WRITE to newspapers in small towns. Ask to have a copy of the newspaper sent to you. Mom can tell you how much money to send to get the paper. You want a paper published about two weeks before you leave. This will give it time to get to you.

STUDY the newspaper carefully. It might give you ideas on interesting places to tour. It should list fairs.

Trip Table

FIND a heavy cardboard box. Get one about 18 inches long and 12 inches wide. It should be 12 inches high.

CUT the flaps off the top. Leave the bottom ones in place. Cut a kneehole along one long side of the top. It should fit over your lap.

GLUE the flaps you cut off around the sides of the bottom. This makes the bottom the table top. The flaps should make one-inch walls around the table top.

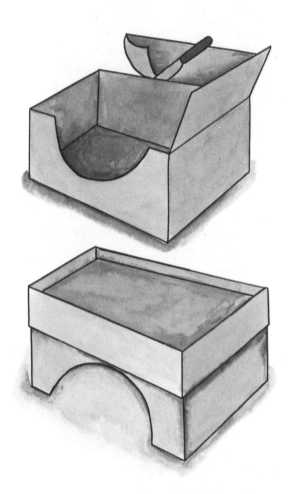

DECORATE the trip table with pictures of airplanes, ships, cars, and trains. Add bicycles, camels, horses, and sleds. Paste on pictures of other ways to travel.

USE the trip table while you ride. It can be a lunch table. Play games on it. Shoot marbles? Unlikely. Use it for a writing desk. Put it between you and your brother if you have a fight. Finger wrestle on it to make up.

Trip Trunk

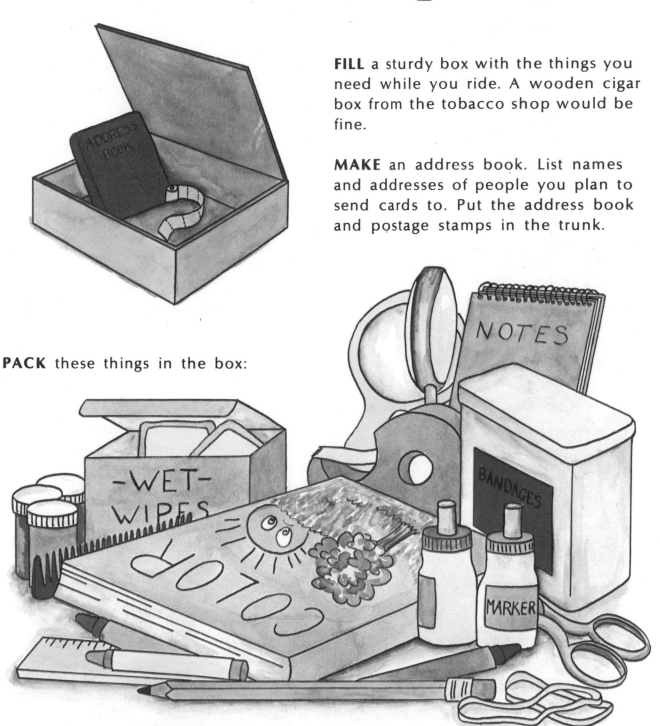

FILL a sturdy box with the things you need while you ride. A wooden cigar box from the tobacco shop would be fine.

MAKE an address book. List names and addresses of people you plan to send cards to. Put the address book and postage stamps in the trunk.

PACK these things in the box:

Thoughts for Food

MAKE some snacks to take in the car.

TRY these Energy Balls.

MIX these things together in a large bowl

       1/2 cup uncooked oatmeal
       1/2 cup finely ground nuts
       1 cup tiny chocolate chips

BLEND

       1/2 cup of peanut butter
       1 tablespoon honey

PUT the peanut butter-honey mixture into the dry ingredients.

MIX the stuff together by cutting through it with a large spoon. Do it lots of times. It will get lumpy.

CHILL the dough for one hour.

WASH and DRY your hands.

FORM one-inch balls out of the dough using your hands.

PUT some wheat germ in a shallow dish. No wheat germ? Use cereal crumbs. Put any kind of flaky cereal in a plastic bag. Press out the air. Tie the bag with a wire twist. Crush the cereal with a rolling pin.

ROLL each ball in the wheat germ or crumbs. Make sure each ball is coated.

POUR milk over the dough that wouldn't form balls. Eat it for a quick snack.

PUT all the balls in a plastic dish with a cover.

STORE the balls in a cool spot in the car.

You could use raisins or coconut instead of chocolate chips. Try sesame seeds.

ANOTHER THOUGHT

PREPARE Snackebabs for your trip.

GET some round toothpicks.

SET UP an assembly line of kids. Give each one a different kind of snack.

USE raisins, pieces of dried fruit, holey cereal, and holey candy. Use tiny marshmallows and small gumdrops.

START with gumdrops. Put one on one end of a toothpick.

PASS the toothpick to the next guy. He adds a piece of his snack and passes the toothpick on.

KEEP ADDING to the toothpick until it is full.

PUT another gumdrop on the other end to hold all the snacks on the toothpick.

PUT all the Snackebabs in a plastic bag.

STORE them in a cool spot in the car.

GET RID of the toothpicks when you've eaten all the tidbits.

No splinters in the throat on this trip—do you mind?

Picky Packer

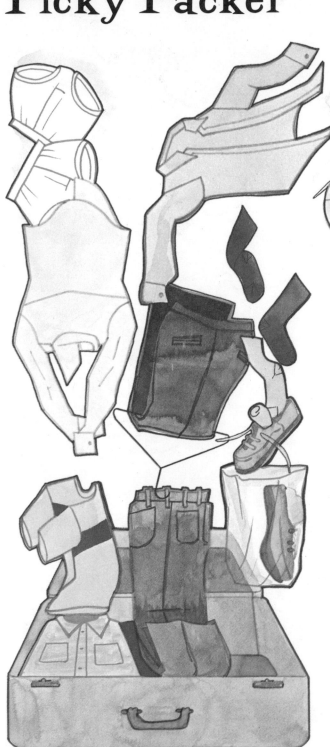

FIGURE OUT how much clothing you need. Take only what is necessary. You probably won't need a tuxedo or ball gown. You can leave your three-foot sombrero at home.

USE one large suitcase.

MARK your own clothes. Use your favorite color of thread. Sew a small X on each piece of clothing. Do put it where it won't show.

PACK dresses, shirts and slacks with their hangers. Fold them in half or in thirds. Layer them neatly in the suitcase.

STUFF shoes with socks, hankies, and underwear. Put the shoes in plastic bags. Roll pajamas and nightgowns. Alternate shoes and nightwear in the suitcase.

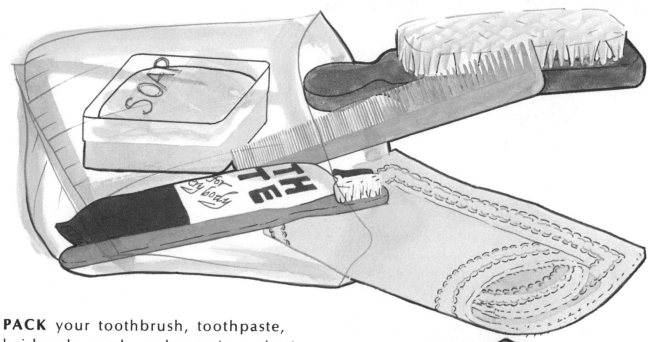

PACK your toothbrush, toothpaste, hairbrush, comb, and soap in a plastic bag. Put the bag in the suitcase.

MAKE a list of all the things you packed. Tape it to the inside of the suitcase.

CHECK the list when it's time to come home. Make sure you have everything.

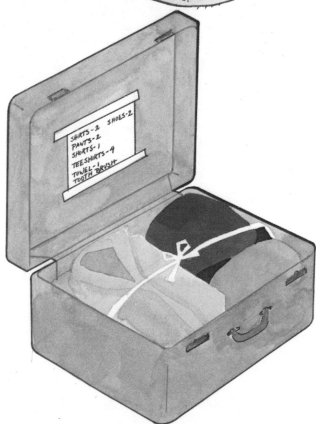

TAKE a big plastic bag for dirty clothes. Put your soiled clothes in it each night. Mixing clean and dirty clothes won't do.

KEEP your suitcase tidy.

CARRY only clothes and simple toilet things in your bag. Liquids can make a mess in luggage.

Goodbye, House.

MAKE your house safe while you are away.

TELL the police what dates your house will be empty. They can check it for you.

CANCEL newspapers while you are gone.

VISIT the post office. Ask the clerk to hold the family's mail until your return.

ASK a neighbor to turn on different lights in your house every night. She might adjust shades or draperies also. Make the house look like someone is there. This same neighbor might water plants for you. Are you leaving your pets at home? They need food, water, and exercise. Ask a good friend to be their caretaker.

FIND someone to keep the lawn trimmed.

TURN OFF all lights the day you leave.

HELP mom clean out the refrigerator before you leave. That nice firm cucumber will turn into a long, green prune, left on its own.

TAKE a house key to your good neighbor. Leave her a note with your car license number, car make and model on it. Write down all the states you will be touring. Give her a telephone number, if possible, where your family can be reached.

Mrs. Carmichael:
our CAR LICENSE #
LLC 356
CHEVROLET IMPALA
STATION WAGON
2-TONE BLUE
We will visit:
MAINE, VERMONT,
NEW HAMPSHIRE
In case of emergencies
Uncle Deke Green will
know exactly where we are
His number is LM3-467

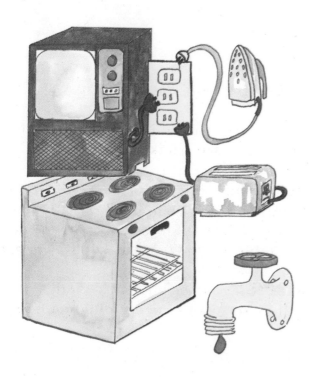

Or.

GIVE the neighbor the number of a close family member. She can call this person in case of emergency.

UNPLUG all appliances including the TV. Make sure all burners and the oven are turned off.

REMIND dad to turn off the outside water taps from the inside of the house.

Is it time to leave?

Back Seat Rider

ARRANGE your back seat space.

SET your trip table on the seat next to you. Your trip trunk could go under it.

PUT a small pillow for napping on the table top. Rest your head on it when you get sleepy. Store the pillow under the table when you are wide awake.

KEEP all your small items in the trunk. Stash away everything not being used.

STORE books, games and you-name-it in a cargo net.

KEEP your snack bar on the floor. A picnic jug of drinkables, paper cups, and snacks can ride by your feet. Don't step on the snacks. Squish.

KEEP the deck behind the back seat cleared off. Clothes stacked up there might interfere with the driver's vision. Playing cards left there could get caught in the wind—and grand slam your father.

He could get angry.

65

Nifty Gifts

MAKE your mother a travel sewing kit.

THREAD six sewing needles with six shades of thread. Use black, white, blue, red, yellow, and green. Push the needles through a small square of paper. Wind the thread around the needles in a figure 8.

WRAP extra thread of each color around an empty thread spool. Keep the thread in place with a strip of clear tape.

GET a cap from a hairspray can. Cover a steel wool scouring pad with a piece of cloth. Pin the edges of the cloth together. Press the pad into the cap. The pinned side goes down. Add straight and safety pins to this pincushion.

STRING different sizes of buttons on a large safety pin.

PUT all these things plus small scissors and a thimble into a small plastic box.

GIFT-WRAP it for mom with fabric and yarn.

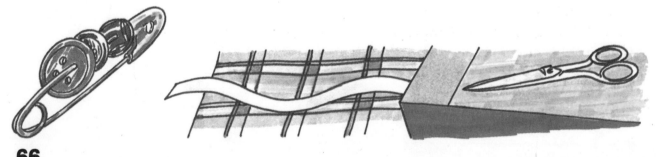

MAKE a map pack for your dad.

GET a piece of vinyl cloth 27 inches square. Fold it so that the doubled part is 12 inches by 27 inches. There will be a 3 inch flap left over.

PUNCH small holes down the edges through the folded part. Make the holes 1/2 inch apart. Measure in 9 inches from each edge. Mark the 9 inch places at three spots. Connect the marks with your pencil to make a line. Punch holes every 1/2 inch along the lines.

UNFOLD the cloth. Sew a button halfway between each row of holes. The buttons should be 4 inches from the top edge.

CUT through the flap to the 9 inch points. Round off each of the three flaps you now have. Sew a button in the center of each flap.

FOLD the cloth again.

SEW the sides of the pack together. Use heavy cord. Put the cord through the first hole. Tie a knot.

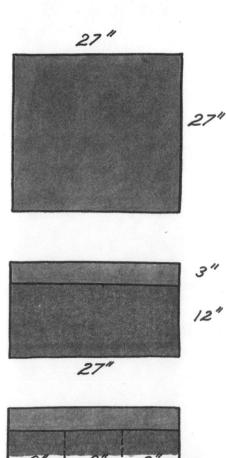

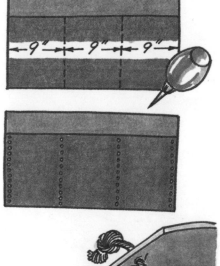

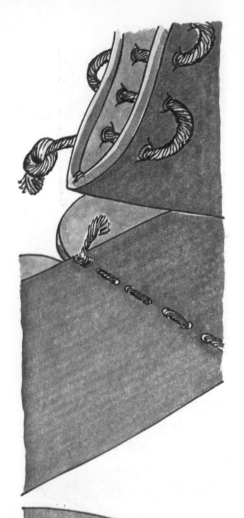

BRING the cord over the edge and through the next hole. Keep going. Tie a knot at the last hole. Do the other side.

SEW the middle seams. Make a knot for the first hole. Weave the cord down through one hole and up through the next. Tie knots at the ends.

CUT three pieces of string 15 inches long. Tie one piece around each button on the front of the pack. Wind the string between those buttons and the flap buttons. This will keep the flaps in place.

FOLD the right pocket over the center one. Fold the left over the right.

PUT maps in one pocket. A large pad of paper will fit in another. Add a pen. The third pocket can hold tour books or receipts.

PUT the map pack and sewing kit on the front seat before you leave.

Surely you have earned a hug for all this work.

Pet Preparations

TAKE a good, honest look at your pet. Decide if he is up to a trip. A strong, healthy pet will do fine. An elderly or nervous pet will have a hard time. Don't take a pet that is recovering from an illness. Puppies do best at home.

CALL a family meeting. Discuss the kinds of places you will visit. Pets prefer an outdoor vacation. Long hikes and camping are great. Pets won't enjoy a trip to the city. They are not welcome in restaurants, museums, or movies.

GET OUT all the guides and pamphlets you collected. Check what they say about pets. Many motels and hotels allow pets. Some even provide kennels. Don't take your pet where he isn't welcome. National Parks allow pets. They must be on a leash at all times. They are not allowed in restaurants or on swimming beaches. Regulations in state parks vary. Often pets must be on a leash. At night they must be in your tent or car. Visit your librarian. She will give you addresses for the parks you will visit.

PLAN a trip to your vet. He will make sure your pet is healthy. Ask for all the necessary shots. Your vet will fill out a health certificate. Ask if your pet may have tranquilizers for the trip.

PREPARE for a trip to Canada. A cat will be checked at the border. He will be allowed in Canada if he is healthy. A dog must have a health certificate. It must show that he had a rabies shot within the last year.

PLAN well in advance for a trip to Mexico. Both dogs and cats must have rabies and distemper shots. Get two copies of a health certificate from your vet. It must have your name, address, and your pet's description. The vet must sign it himself and include the date. Hurry down to the library. Ask the librarian for the address of the nearest Mexican Consulate. Send in the health certificate. The consulate will return the proper papers and charge a fee.

BRING a pet into the United States. Cats will be checked at the border. A healthy cat may cross the border. A dog will be checked too. He must have a rabies certificate.

Tag Him

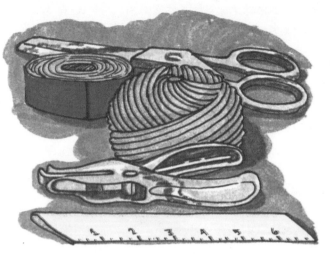

My owner's name is:
Bonnie Ward
29801 Maplegrove
Any City, U.S.A.
201-3384

In emergency, call:
John Ward
29801 Maplegrove
Any City, U.S.A.
201-3384

FIND wide cloth tape, heavy paper, string, pen, scissors, ruler, hole punch, and hair spray.

TAKE OFF your pet's collar. Cut a piece of tape twice as wide as the collar. Make it about two inches long.

SET the tape on the table sticky side up. Cut out two pieces of paper to fit on the tape. Press them onto the tape.

WRITE your name, address, and phone number on the top paper. Find out who will handle family emergencies. Write that person's name, address, and phone number on the bottom piece. Leave room at both ends of the papers to punch holes.

SPRAY both papers with hair spray.

FOLD over the tape. Write your pet's name on the outside. Spray it with hair spray.

PUNCH two holes on each end of the tag. Don't punch through any of the writing.

CUT OFF two lengths of thin, strong string. Put each string through the holes.

TIE the tag onto the collar. Make a strong knot that won't come off. Cut off the extra string.

Pet Practice

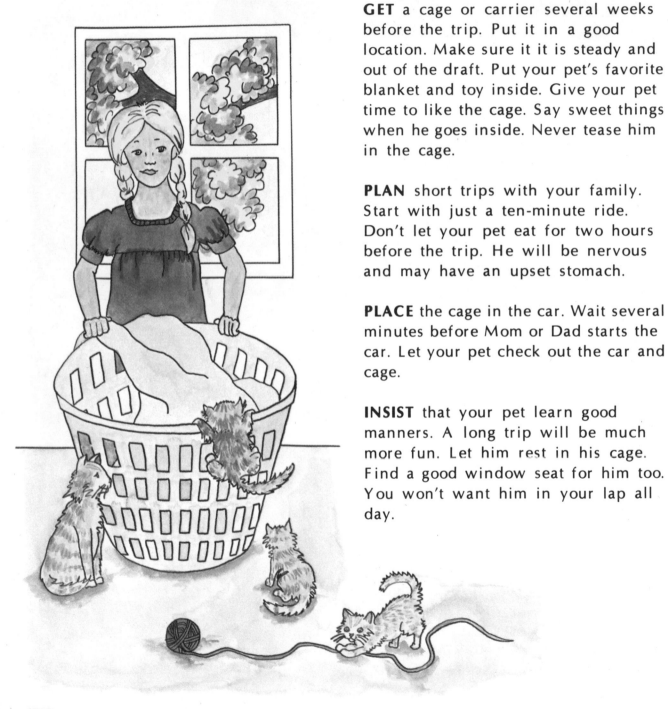

GET a cage or carrier several weeks before the trip. Put it in a good location. Make sure it it is steady and out of the draft. Put your pet's favorite blanket and toy inside. Give your pet time to like the cage. Say sweet things when he goes inside. Never tease him in the cage.

PLAN short trips with your family. Start with just a ten-minute ride. Don't let your pet eat for two hours before the trip. He will be nervous and may have an upset stomach.

PLACE the cage in the car. Wait several minutes before Mom or Dad starts the car. Let your pet check out the car and cage.

INSIST that your pet learn good manners. A long trip will be much more fun. Let him rest in his cage. Find a good window seat for him too. You won't want him in your lap all day.

Pack It

PLACE the cage or carrier in the car. Make sure it is steady and out of people's way. The door must open easily without rearranging the whole back seat. Put a familiar blanket and toy inside.

FIND a safe place for the health certificate. Put it with your family's other important papers. Or make a special case for the certificate.

WEDGE a water dish in a spot where it won't tip. Fill it part way with water. Take along a thermos with more water.

FIND a snack or small box. Pack what your pet needs. Include a leash, bowls, comb, brush, dry food, canned food, can opener, and some treats.

CONSIDER a litter box for a cat. Put newspapers under the box. Line it with a disposable plastic bag.

On the Way

MAKE SURE your pet always has fresh water. Fill up the thermos at gas stops.

EXERCISE your pet whenever possible. Take him for a brisk walk just before the trip starts. Try to stop for a short walk every hour. Always walk him on a leash.

KEEP your pet inside a moving car. He may like hanging out his head, but it isn't good for him. Dirt and grime will irritate his eyes and nose. The wind may cause infections in his ears or throat.

COOL your pet. A parked car gets hot very quickly. Ask the driver to park in the shade. Open every window just far enough so the pet can't get out. Try staying in the car with your pet. Imagine how hot you would be in a fur coat.

WATCH OUT for cat claws. A cat will be nervous for the first few rides. Keep him in a cage or on a leash. A jump on the driver's neck is dangerous.

Motel Manners

TREAT your neighbors with consideration. Keep your pet quiet during the night. A sleeping spot near you may help. Keep messes off the sidewalks. Take your pet for a walk in the woods or grass.

KEEP a motel room in good condition. Don't leave your pet alone. He may scratch, claw, and howl. Clean up spilled food, empty cans, and other garbage.

DON'T LOSE a pet. Open the outside door carefully. Keep your pet on a leash when he is outside.

FEED him an early breakfast. Eating two hours before the trip will settle your pet's stomach. Take a good walk just before you start driving.

CONSIDER your neighbors in a campground. They appreciate good manners too.

*Purr...*fection

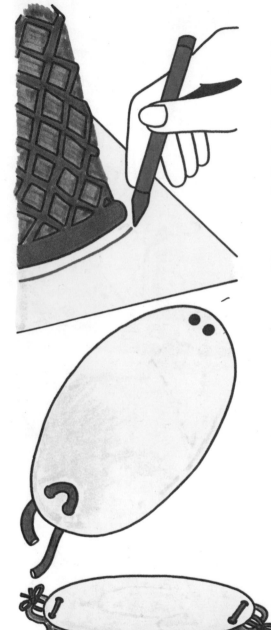

FIND a very large laundry basket, heavy cardboard, and strong rope. Use a pencil and a strong knife.

TURN the basket upside down on the cardboard. Draw a line around the basket. Take away the basket. Draw another line about half an inch inside the first one.

CUT the cardboard along the inside line. Be careful. It's easy to cut fingers or to cut through the carpet.

SET the cardboard on top of the basket. Check to see how it fits. Trim off the extra cardboard. Strong scissors will do the job.

MARK the location for four holes in the cardboard. Put two at each end. The cardboard must remain strong. Make the holes at least two inches from the edge. Leave at least two inches between the holes.

CUT OFF two lengths of rope. Put them through the holes. Tie the lid to the handles on the basket.

GET some shredded foam and some cloth. An old bath towel is fine. Use pins, needle, scissors, pencil, and thread.

SET the basket on the cloth. Draw a line around the edge of the basket. Cut along the line.

PLACE the cut cloth on top of another piece. Smooth out the wrinkles. Pin it in place. Cut along the edge of the first piece of cloth.

THREAD the needle with strong thread. Stitch around the cloth about half an inch inside the edge. Leave about six inches unstitched. Tie a knot at the end of the stitches.

REMOVE the pins. Turn the cloth right side out.

FILL the cushion with shredded foam.

THREAD the needle again. Fold in the edges of cloth. Stitch the seam shut.

PLACE the cushion in the bottom of the laundry basket.

FIND some strong string and an empty plastic container. A dish detergent bottle is just the right size. Give it a good cleaning.

DRAW a line around the bottle. Make it about 2-1/2 inches from the bottom. Draw a flap on one side.

CUT the bottle along the line. Remember to leave the flap attached.

POKE two holes in the flap.

CUT OFF a piece of string. Put it through the holes. Attach the dish inside the laundry basket.

KEEP food or treats inside the dish. Watch your cat try to pull out pieces of dry food.

Freeway Fun

Window Watchers

SIT so that each person has a good view from the window. Look for billboards, mailboxes, and signs. Call out the letter A when you see it. Start looking for a B. Allow only one letter for each sign. Take the letters in order. The person who finishes the alphabet first is the winner.

PLAY the same game using objects instead of letters. Use an ambulance or an artichoke for A.

LOOK at the parts of your car. Think of parts you can't see. The first player names a part for A, such as air valve. The second player names a part for B. Continue until you finish the alphabet.

ASK an adult to make a list of animals you may see. Give point values to the animals. Give one point to very common animals. Give ten points to an animal you probably won't see. Make two lists of the animals. Write the point value next to each animal. Divide yourselves into two groups. Each group gets a different side of the road. Write down the points each time you see an animal. Try to get the most points for your group.

ASK one person to play with you. Watch the oncoming cars. One person counts all the two-door cars. The other person counts all the four-door cars. The person who reaches 25 first is the winner.

TRY to find all the numbers from 1 to 100. The numbers must be found in order. Look for numbers on signs. Count groups of objects. Five cows in a pasture count for the number five. The winner reaches 100 first.

More Watchers

WATCH out the window for pairs of things. Find two suitcases, two horses, or anything in pairs. Only pairs count. The person who reaches twenty pairs first is the winner.

ASK each person to choose a different color. Say "Paint it" and your color each time you see a car in your color. Give yourself five points each time you say "Paint it." The person who reaches 100 points first is the winner.

ASK one person to play with you. Each person chooses one side of the road. Give yourself a point each time you see an animal. Give yourself five points for a napping cat. See who has the most points after five minutes.

REMEMBER something you just saw along the road. Give everyone a clue such as its size or color. Someone must guess what it is before you go two miles.

THINK of something you'll probably see along the road. The first person to see it gets a point. Give each person half a point for a tie. Think of something else you'll see. The winner has the most points when the car stops.

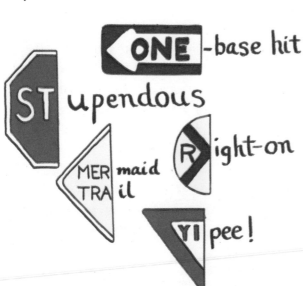

PRETEND that each sign is only half a sign. Think of a good line for the second half.

PLAY any game by yourself. See how many points you can get in ten miles.

License Listers

LNDAZPYS
LP

1. LAZY
2. DAYS
3. PLAY

KLM-221

PLAY with one other person. Watch the oncoming cars. One person counts the license plates that end in odd numbers. The other person counts even numbers. Try to get the most plates in five minutes. Play again. This time add two points for out-of-state plates.

LOOK for license plates with letters. Write down the first ten letters you see. Make as many words from the letters as you can. Use each letter only once. Try again with twenty letters.

MAKE a contest from out-of-state plates. Name the state as soon as you can. Give a point to the first correct guesser. Subtract a point from each wrong guesser's score. Count only the top plates on a truck.

SEARCH for numbers in order. Find 1, then 2, then 3 and so on. The numbers after nine are harder to find. Play alone or play with your brother. See who can get to fifty first.

PICK a number that has four digits. For example, take 7694. Give yourself one point for finding it scrambled, such as 9647. Give yourself five points for finding the numbers in order. Try to get ten points before lunch.

CHOOSE any word you like. Spell it out in license plates. Look for the first letter. Then go on to the next letter. The letters must be found in order.

WATCH for the first license plate with three letters. Write down the letters. See who can write the longest word with those letters in it.

Mad Mappers

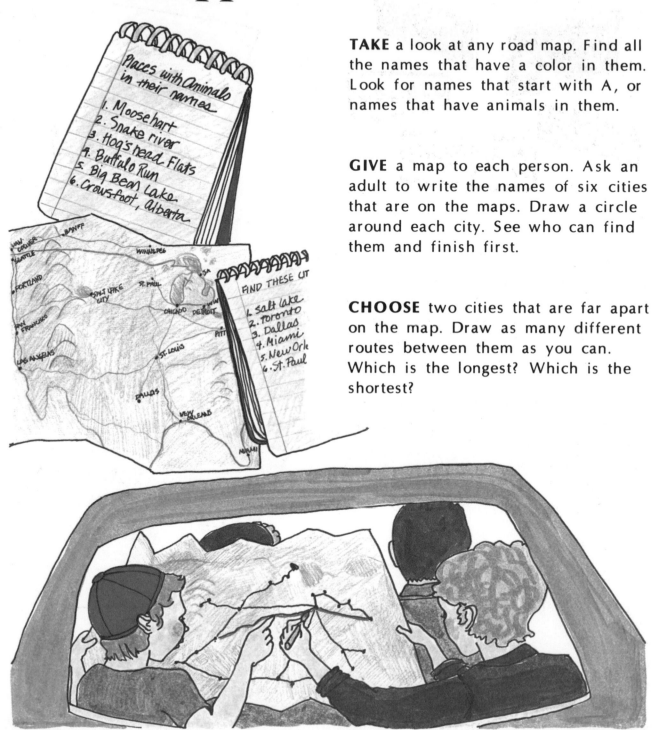

TAKE a look at any road map. Find all the names that have a color in them. Look for names that start with A, or names that have animals in them.

GIVE a map to each person. Ask an adult to write the names of six cities that are on the maps. Draw a circle around each city. See who can find them and finish first.

CHOOSE two cities that are far apart on the map. Draw as many different routes between them as you can. Which is the longest? Which is the shortest?

GET OUT the map for the area you are traveling. Find your road. Choose a town or other landmark ahead. Guess what time you will arrive at that place. Ask each person to write down his guess. Wait to see who is closest.

OPEN a map between two people. One player chooses a place on the map. He says, "I see a lake beginning with H," or "I see a city beginning with S." The other player has two minutes to find the place. He can put his finger on the map. The other player says "hot" or "cold." Take turns choosing a place on the map.

WRITE down a list of things you can remember from a map. Try states—or states east of the Mississippi. Think of one state and name the states that border it. Try to list capitals, cities, rivers, or lakes. Look at a map to check your list.

TABLE TRIPPERS

WRITE down the names of several places. Put each name into a silly sentence. Illustrate the silliest.

Jolly John picked a <u>bathtub</u> of <u>cherry</u> <u>vans</u> in <u>Vancouver</u> today.

CHOOSE a long name from a map. Write it down on a piece of paper. Put one letter on each line. Think of something you have seen on the trip that begins with the first letter. Write it after the letter. Continue until you have something for each letter.

Horned toad
Oats
University
Geyser
Hurricane
Totem pole
Owl
Niagara Falls

Visit Grannys' rugged hotel for the best air-conditioned free hamburger.

FIND ten words from billboards. Take only one word from each billboard. Write all ten words into one sentence.

GET OUT a large sheet of paper. Draw a farm. Include the barn, silo, fences, and fields. Draw in the animals only when you see them from the window.

CHOOSE something that you just saw. Draw the first part of it. Fold the paper to cover what you drew. Pass the paper to the next person. Let him draw the next part, fold the paper, and pass it on. Open the paper after everyone has had a turn.

DRAW a card with twenty-five squares on it. Give a card to each person. Tell each to draw an animal in the center square. Everyone must have a different animal. Draw an X in a square each time you see your animal. The first person to fill up all the squares wins. Think of other categories for the center square. Let each person choose a different category.

Sweet Silence

GET a pencil and paper. Ask someone to time five minutes for you. Write down all the sounds you hear. Compare your list with someone else's.

ASK the driver to tell you when to start. Sit quietly and try to judge when a mile has gone by. Raise your hand when you think you've gone a mile. The driver will tell you who was closest.

CHOOSE someone to be the leader. He will do silent actions such as rub his head and pat his stomach. Copy all his actions except when a car is passing. You are out if you copy an action while a car is passing. The last one out is the new leader.

ASK the driver to measure three miles. Choose a leader. He will do any silent thing to make you laugh. Try not to laugh or make a sound for three miles. Choose a new leader.

PRETEND there is a travel trunk in the back seat. Choose some piece of clothing from it and describe it in mime. People will guess what it is. They will write their guesses on small pieces of paper. Check all the guesses. The first right guesser will choose something else from the trunk.

GIVE a piece of paper to each person. Tell him to write something silly to act out. Put all the papers in a bag. One person will choose a paper and act it out. The others must not laugh or make a sound. Let each person take a turn acting out.

Finger Flappers

HOLD your hands in front of you, fingers closed, thumbs out. Move one thumb in a forward circle. Move the other thumb in a backward circle. Move both thumbs at the same time.

HOLD OUT one hand. Open and close the second and third fingers like a scissors. Try moving the second finger and holding the third finger stiff. Try moving the third finger and holding the second stiff.

MAKE a large 6 in the air with your finger. Make a zero with your toe. Do both at the same time.

PUT the tips of your thumb and third finger on one hand together. Place your second finger in the circle. Wiggle your second finger.

Muscle Movers

HOLD UP your elbows. Grasp your hands together with the fingers. Try to pull your hands apart.

SIT straight with your knees together. Place your hands between your knees. Try to hold your knees together with your legs. At the same time, try to pull them apart with your hands.

SIT straight with your eyes closed and hands in your lap. Concentrate on your feet and toes. Tighten your foot muscles, then relax them. Concentrate on your lower leg. Tighten the muscles, then relax them. Move up through all your body muscles. Relax your whole body. Drop your chin forward. Roll your head slowly in a circle.

Cargo Net

DECIDE where to hang your cargo net. Ask the driver. He won't want to see a cargo net in the mirror. Put it in a safe place. It shouldn't flop in your eye. Measure about how long your net will be.

FIND two strong rings. Your Mom's old bracelets are just the right size.

GET a ruler, scissors, rubberbands, tape, and strong string. Jute or string for packages is fine. Look for good colors.

CUT OFF a piece of cord six times the length of your cargo net. Use it to measure more cords the same length. Cut a total of eighteen cords.

FOLD each cord in half. Remember how to make a lark's head. Attach each cord to the ring with a lark's head.

WIND UP each cord from the bottom. Put a rubberband around it. Short cords tangle less.

PLACE the ring on your lap board. Tape down the ring to hold it in place.

REMEMBER how to tie square knots.

COUNT out four cords on the left side. Push the others out of your way. Tie two square knots.

COUNT out another four cords. Tie two more square knots. Keep working until all the cords are tied in knots.

REMEMBER how to tie alternate square knots.

BEGIN another row of knots. Count out two cords on the left side. Push them out of the way. Count out four more cords. Tie two square knots. Keep working across the row. Two cords will be left over.

LOOK at your two rows of knots. One row uses all the cords. The other row has two cords left over on each end. Do one row and then the other. Leave about half an inch space between the rows. Keep working until the cargo net is as long as you want it. End with the row that uses all the cords.

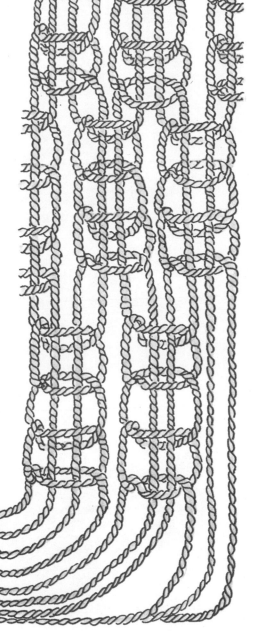

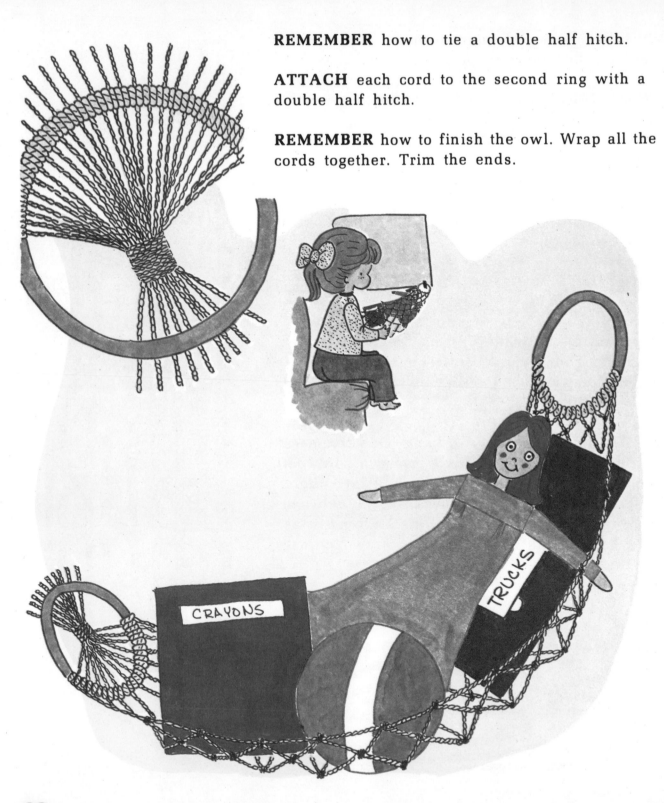

REMEMBER how to tie a double half hitch.

ATTACH each cord to the second ring with a double half hitch.

REMEMBER how to finish the owl. Wrap all the cords together. Trim the ends.

CRAYONS

TRUCKS

HERE

TO

THERE

Top Security

BE a good passenger—ride safely.

USE your seat belts. Pretend they are parachute straps. Or that you are a racing car driver. Anything you like. It is your imagination.

STAY SEATED. Standing, climbing or jumping are things to do at a park.

KEEP all your body parts inside the car. The only thing going into and out of car windows should be air.

TALK or SING in quiet voices. Shrieks or screams can startle the driver. Who wants to spend a vacation in a ditch?

KEEP your hands to yourself. Don't touch the driver. Your hands must stay away from the steering wheel, gearshift, and radio.

PUT AWAY any sharp things. Quick stops can send them flying. Ouch.

KEEP magnifying glasses and mirrors in their cases. They can cause fires if left in sunlight.

SAVE quarrels and horsing around for a later time.

LOCK the car each time the family gets out.

PUT all valuable things in the trunk. They shouldn't be left on seats where they can be seen.

STAY with your family when you get out of the car. Don't get wanderlost.

OFFER to be the Inspector. Check the car's headlights when you get out. Be sure they are off.

MAKE SURE the driver has the car keys before he locks the car.

WATCH the gas gauge. Tell the driver before it reaches the empty mark.

TELL the driver if you think a tire is soft.

Woozy Rider

TAKE along some throw-away helpers if you get carsick.

CUT the top off a half-gallon milk carton. Wash out the carton. Line it with a plastic bag. Take extra bags and wire ties for them.

USE the carton if you feel ill and the car can't stop. Dispose of the bag as soon as possible.

KEEP some premoistened towelettes for cleaning up. They also feel good on a hot forehead.

RIDE in the front seat if you can. Look out the front window instead of the side windows. This might help.

EAT lightly. Get as much fresh air as you can while riding. Frequent rest stops will help.

Have you thought about traveling by jinrikisha?

Feeling Fine

TRAVEL healthy. Stay in good shape on your trip.

EAT balanced meals. Too many snacks can give you a very efficient stomach ache. So can spoiled food. Tell mom if you think your food tastes funny.

GET plenty of rest.

WEAR your shoes everywhere except at the beach. Tourists are sometimes careless with bottles and cans.

PROTECT yourself from sunburn. Use a sunscreen lotion. Wear a shirt to keep your back from cooking.

PLUNK a hat on your head if you are going to be walking in the sun for a long time. How about sunglasses?

KEEP long hair in braids or bundled into a hat while riding at amusement parks.

WEAR insect repellent. No bites, thanks anyway. Stay away from poison ivy and its friends.

Elegant Behavior

BE a polite traveler.

USE indoor voices in restaurants. Go to the bathroom quietly after you have ordered. No loud announcement about it. Frankly, no one else is interested.

SPEAK to dad about a soiled spoon or cracked drinking glass. He will ask the waitress for a different one.

BE PATIENT. Special places or events are usually crowded.

STAY happy. Avoid getting cross. Wait for your turn. Don't cut into lines.

MAKE friends with someone else who is waiting in line. Chat about your dog or your trip. Swap fishing stories.

THROW waste paper from treats or souvenirs into trash receptacles. Help keep the place tidy for other visitors.

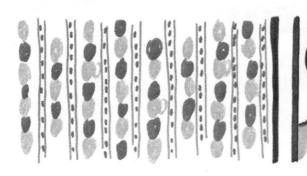

BE a model motel guest. Walk in the corridors. No running.

DON'T KNOCK on the other guests' doors as you pass them.

MOVE quietly in your room. This is really important if you are not on the first floor.

KEEP the television and radio volumes down low.

OBEY all motel rules. Follow the pool rules carefully.

BE CAREFUL about repacking your suitcase. Make sure no towels or glasses from the motel go out with you.

USE "Please" and "Thank-you" at the right times. Add "You are welcome" and "Excuse me" when needed.

STOP at the motel or hotel manager's office when you leave. Tell him what a nice time you had.

You did, of course.

Noble Navigator

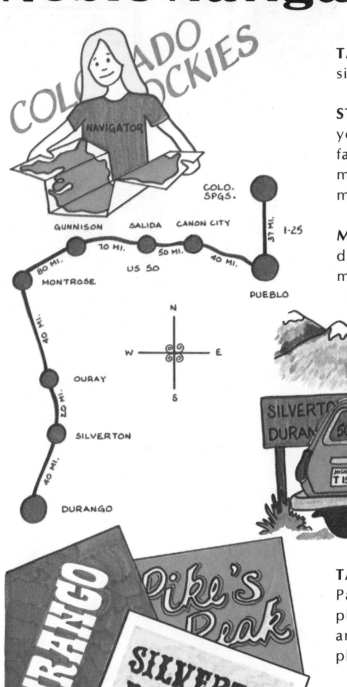

TAKE TURNS being the navigator. He sits next to the driver.

STUDY the map the night before it's your turn. Figure out how far the family will travel the next day. Use the map legend to judge the number of miles.

MAKE sectional maps for the next day's travel. Copy from the original map.

TALK with the Keeper of the Pamphlets. Find out what special places will be visited. Study pamphlets and maps to see how to get to these places.

BE ABLE to tell the driver how far away the next town is.

FIND OUT about any detours or construction zones. Maps sometimes show these.

CALL the highway patrol or auto club before you leave home. Ask for detour information. Write down all the facts.

Navigating is a big responsibility.

Logbook Keeper

BUY a medium-sized notebook. Tape a pocket on the inside cover to hold a pencil. Make it large enough to hold post cards to be mailed.

MAKE columns on each page. Use a left and right page for each day of the trip.

LABEL the left page columns
>Date
>Odometer Reading
>Towns
>Special Notes

The odometer is a dial on the dashboard. It shows how many miles the car has gone.

LIST all the towns you pass through each day. Write any unusual things you did or saw under Special Notes.

LABEL the right page columns
    Breakfast
    Lunch
    Dinner
    Lodging
    Car Costs
    Other Expenses

WRITE after each meal the place where you ate and the cost. Do the same for lodging. Jot down where dad stopped for gas and how much it cost. List other expenses.

ADD UP each day's costs when you stop for the night. Fill in the odometer reading at the end of the day. Subtract the first reading from the second reading. This tells you how many miles you traveled that day.

SHARE the job of logbook keeper with brothers and sisters.

Today we went to Eagle Canyon. It was sunny. We drove 2?? miles.

Using a real log for keeping notes would be rather heavy, don't you think?

109

Perfect Passenger

FIND ways to help the trip go smoother.

OFFER to amuse younger brothers or sisters. Make up stories to tell them. Use their names in the stories. Build stories around things they do. See how long it takes them to start adding to the story.

PLAY with the wiggly baby. Mom's lap gets tired. Take the baby into the back seat with you. Sing to him. Give him his bottle. Let him nap on your lap.

BE the car custodian.

PUT AWAY games and toys after playing. Keep small things in boxes so they won't get lost.

COLLECT all the scraps of paper, used tissue and other waste stuff. Dump it all into the litter bag. Or any paper bag.

SWEEP OUT the car with a whisk broom.

DAMPEN a paper towel. Dust the dashboard and the deck behind the back seat.

EMPTY the ashtrays. Dump the litter bag into a waste can. Put the bag back in its place.

USE a wet paper towel to clean the windows in the back. Clean off fingerprints, lipprints, and noseprints.

CLEAN UP any sticky messes that happened during the day.

REFOLD the maps and put them in the map pack.

EMPTY the juice container. Wash it out. Tomorrow you can refill it with juice or ice water.

TURN somersaults from one end of the motel lawn to the other when you get there.

SKIP the same distance if there is no grass for somersaulting.

VAGABOND VALUABLES

COLLECT things on your trip.

FILL pill bottles with soil from different places on your journey. Label each bottle.

PUT pretty stones or seashells in other bottles. Label these also.

STORE on-the-ground-I-found prizes in small boxes. Things like leaves, feathers, or tiny pine cones. You know better than to pick things, of course.

KEEP paper placemats from restaurants.

SAVE paper napkins, toothpick packs, and matchbook covers. Give the matches to dad.

GET as many postcards as you can. Mail some to friends or relatives. Buy two of the ones you like best. Mail one. Keep one for yourself. Bring home postcards from each state.

USE envelopes to save all the paper things you collect. Label each. Tell what is in it and where you got it.

KEEP all the things you collect in a flat box.

ASK dad if you can store the box under the front seat.

PROTECT the box from the baby.

PROTECT the baby from the box.

Economy Run

MAKE a list of ways to travel using the least amount of money.

THINK about meals. Look at the prices you got from restaurants. You can see that some places charge more than others.

CHOOSE restaurants that are cheaper but serve good food. Order only what you can eat. Let mom and dad decide when to eat more expensively.

EAT in department store cafeterias.

CHECK prices in motel restaurants. It might be better to go somewhere else to dine.

PACK supplies to have one or two picnics each day.

BREAKFAST at a roadside park at dawn. Small boxes of cereal, milk, sugar and fresh oranges taste good outside. Watch nature wake up.

BUY food at a grocery store to make lunch. Eat in a city or state park. This is a good chance to play and exercise. One-two-three and four.

WEAR comfortable clothes for traveling. They don't have to be new. New clothes just get pruny from riding in them. Save your new things for special events.

USE self-operated laundries. This is cheaper than having the motel staff do your laundry.

BUDGET spending money. Spend only so much each day. Decide whether to get lots of little souvenirs or one big one.

TAKE snacks along in the car. Stopping for snacks costs more than you think.

BRING along a container of ice water. Add frozen lemonade or fruit punch.

STOP at parks for between-meal munchery.

CHECK the motel prices you got before leaving home. The higher-priced ones have things like swimming pools or tennis courts. It is the parents' decision about how much to spend on hotels and motels. Don't whine if you can't swim every night.

STAY in small towns overnight. The hotel charges are smaller and the charms larger.

SPEND some nights in tourist homes. These are also cheaper. Some farms accept paying guests.

PACK everything you need for the trip. Avoid having to buy things that you forgot to take.

You might want to be the cost accountant for next year's vacation.

Think about it.

COMIN'
HOME

Roamers' Return

ZOOM OUT of the car when it stops in your driveway. Race up and down to get the kinks out.

GO BACK to the car. Help unload things. Take each suitcase to its owner's bedroom. Sports equipment can go straight back to the garage or basement.

PLUG IN all the appliances.

UNPACK your luggage. Put your dirty clothes in the laundry room. Make a separate stack of things that need mending.

OFFER to clean out the cooler. Put it back in storage.

The next day:

EMPTY the car ashtrays. Dust the seats and dashboard. Vacuum or sweep out the car.

CALL the police department. Say that your family is home.

PICK UP all the mail at the post office. Tell the postal clerk that delivery can be started again.

TELL the newspaper carrier that he can start bringing the paper again.

VISIT the neighbors and friends who took such good care of your home and pets.

GIVE them all major thank-you's.

It is good to be sleeping in your own bed again, isn't it?

119

Hi! I'm Back!

LET your friends know you are home. Go visiting.

TAKE a token of your trip to each friend.

USE the picture postcards you brought home. Or draw pictures on plain cards of places you visited.

WRITE a short note on each card. Tell what the picture is about. After the note, write "Here is a sample of earth from (the name of the place)."

PUT small amounts of soil on pieces of cellophane 2 inches by 4 inches. Fold the cellophane to make a two-inch square packet. Tape the edges.

TAPE a soil packet on the card.

USE other kinds of specimens as coming-home gifts.

TAKE the tops or bottoms of small boxes. Line them with pieces of fabric.

TO ALICIA: this is where we had a picnic last Tuesday. Here is a sample of earth from Joy Park. LOVE cindy

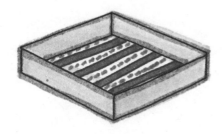

PLACE rocks, dried flowers, or feathers on the fabric. Cover the container with clear food wrap. Tape it in place on the bottom.

LINE some boxes with sandpaper to hold seashells. Cover these with clear food wrap also.

WRITE a small note describing each specimen. Attach the note to the gift.

MAKE a layered soil display with several kinds of earth.

USE a clear pill bottle or small mayonnaise jar.

PUT about one-half inch of soil in the bottom of the bottle. Pack it down firmly. Keep adding and packing until you reach the top of the bottle. The layers must be packed firmly or they will mix.

PLACE the lid on the bottle. Tie a label to the top of the bottle.

Is it heavy enough for a paperweight?

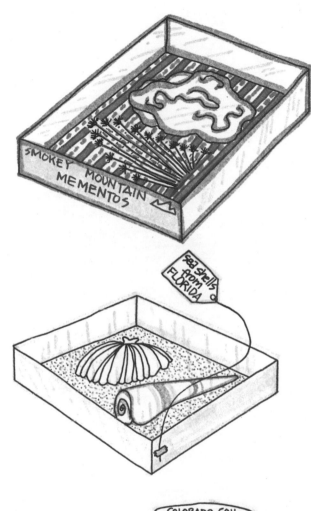

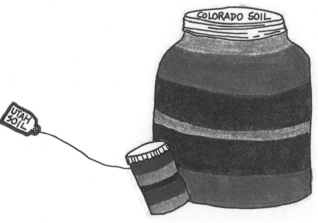

Do a Diorama

MAKE a miniature scene of one part of your vacation.

GET a box about 12 inches square. It can have sides about 4 inches high.

USE sand and earth to form mountains and valleys. Moss can be grass.

COLLECT twigs to make tiny trees.

CUT curved pieces of aluminum foil. Cover them with blue cellophane to make rivers or streams.

ADD rocks or stones. Build a waterfall with them.

MAKE a tiny tent if you were camping. Put it near a river or wherever you camped.

PAINT the inside back of a box blue. Paint the inside sides blue too. (A small tongue-twister there). When the blue dries, paint an ocean liner on the back. Paint clouds on the sides.

PUT about one inch of sand along the front half of the box.

USE foil to make the ocean. Pinch it to make waves.

USE seashells to make sea creatures. Glue on legs made of wire twists. Paint faces on them. Crabby crab. Operatic octopus. Sly shark.

PLACE the creatures on the beach and in the ocean.

SPRINKLE some salt here and there for realism.

GIVE the diorama to one of your grandparents.

Remembering, Sighing

MAKE a memory book about your trip.

GET two pieces of stiff cardboard. They should be about 12 inches square. They will be the covers of your book.

ASK dad or mom to give you a couple of old maps to cut up.

CUT the maps into pieces. Make them different shapes. The pieces should be no bigger than your hand. Make them no smaller than your big toe.

GLUE the pieces of map all over both sides of the covers.

TRIM OFF any map pieces that go beyond the edges of the covers.

CHOOSE which sides of the covers will be on the outside.

THINK of a title for your book. It might be "My Trip." How about "The Cross-Country Traverse of the Jones Family via Motorized Vehicle, Volume I?" Whatever.

CUT the letters for the title out of felt or colored paper. Print the title on the cover the way you want it to look. Space the letters carefully. Glue the cut out letters over the printing.

PUNCH three evenly-spaced holes down the left sides of the covers.

SPRAY the covers inside and out with hairspray. You will ask to borrow the hairspray first, right?

GET some plain paper that measures 8-1/2 by 11 inches. It can be colored or white.

DIVIDE the book into sections for each state you visited. Maybe you would rather divide it by dates.

MAKE section dividers out of some of the paper. Run clear tape down each side of the dividers on the front and back. Punch holes down the left side to match the covers.

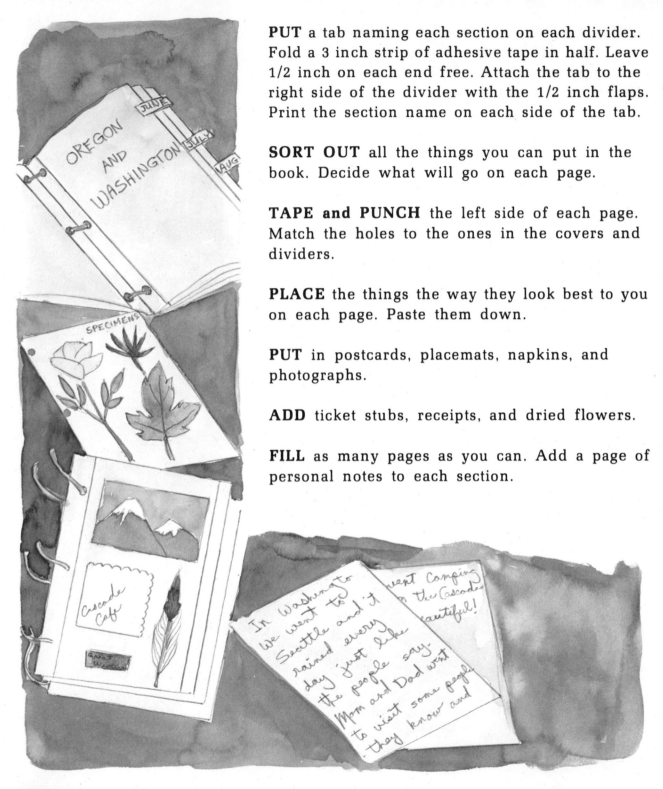

PUT a tab naming each section on each divider. Fold a 3 inch strip of adhesive tape in half. Leave 1/2 inch on each end free. Attach the tab to the right side of the divider with the 1/2 inch flaps. Print the section name on each side of the tab.

SORT OUT all the things you can put in the book. Decide what will go on each page.

TAPE and PUNCH the left side of each page. Match the holes to the ones in the covers and dividers.

PLACE the things the way they look best to you on each page. Paste them down.

PUT in postcards, placemats, napkins, and photographs.

ADD ticket stubs, receipts, and dried flowers.

FILL as many pages as you can. Add a page of personal notes to each section.

GLUE a brown envelope on the inside of the back cover. Put the logbook in the envelope.

NUMBER the pages in the memory book.

BIND the covers, dividers, and pages together.

CUT leather shoestrings into 6 inch pieces. Use one piece for each set of holes. Run the string through the holes. Tie it in a good knot on the outside.

PUT the book away for awhile.

LOOK at it when you are bored or unhappy.

You sure had a good trip, didn't you?

Sigh.